Peach Cookbook

D1472576

0 11557 01165 4

Peach Cookbook

Beverages, Breakfast Treats, Appetizers, Soups, Salads, Sides, Entrées, Desserts

Mimi Brodeur

STACKPOLE BOOKS

First published in paperback in 2012 by
STACKPOLE BOOKS
5067 Ritter Road
Mechanicsburg, PA 17055
www.stackpolebooks.com

Printed in the United States

First paperback edition

10 9 8 7 6 5 4 3 2

Photographs by Alan Wycheck
Food styling by Mimi Brodeur
Cover design by Wendy A. Reynolds

ISBN-13: 978-0-8117-1165-4 (paperback)

Library of Congress Cataloging-in-Publication Data

Brodeur, Mimi.
    Peach cookbook : beverages, breakfast treats, appetizers, soups, salads, entrées, and desserts / Mimi Brodeur. — 1st ed.
        p.   cm.
    Includes index.
    ISBN-13: 978-0-8117-0473-1 (hardcover)
    ISBN-10: 0-8117-0473-4 (hardcover)
        1. Cookery (Peaches) I. Title.
TX813.P4B76   2009
641.6'425—dc22

                                                    2008033765

To my parents,
Ruth and Michael Brodeur,
for the Easy-Bake Oven
that began my culinary endeavors

Contents

Preface   xi

All About Peaches   xiii

Beverages   1

Peachy White Wine Sangria   2
Peach Crantini   4
Sparkling Peach Lemonade   5
Strawberry Peach Smoothie   6
Peach Bellini   7
Peach Sunrise   8

Breakfast Treats   9

Cinnamon Peach Muffins   10
Yogurt with Fresh Peaches and Nutty Granola   12
Lemon Peach Crumb Cake   14
Baked Oatmeal with Peaches and Whipped Cream   16
Fresh Fruit Kabobs   18
Blackberry Peach French Toast   19
Lemon Pound Cake with Fruit Salad   20
Cranberry Orange Scones with Orchard Peach Jam   22
Lemon Ginger Peach Marmalade for Croissants
    or Biscuits   24

Appetizers   25

Peach Bruschetta Topping   26
Sesame Ginger Chicken Skewers with Spicy
    Peach Chipotle Sauce   28
Shiitake Shrimp Peach Tostadas   30
Prosciutto-Wrapped Peaches   32
Peach Guacamole   33
Blackened Scallops with Fresh Peach Sauce
    and Balsamic Reduction   34
Summer-Ripe Salsa   36

Soups, Salads, and Sides   37

Chilled Peach Soup   38
Luscious Crab Peach Salad   39
Peach-Kissed Summer Squash Soup with
    Cilantro Cream   40
Curried Peach Chicken Salad   42
Indian Spiced Lentils with Peaches   43
Peach Salad with Raspberry Vinaigrette   44
Lemon Barley Salad with Peaches   46
Creamy Leeks and Peaches   48
Pine Nut Peach Couscous   50

Entrées   51

Moroccan Peach Lamb Tagine   52
Nut-Crusted Mahimahi with Black Bean Fruit Salsa   54
Mustard-Thyme Chicken Thighs   56
Smoke-Rubbed Skirt Steak with Peach Chive Butter
    and Roasted Rosemary Potatoes   58
Pesto Penne Pasta with Peaches and Grilled
    Summer Vegetables   60
Spicy Pork Babyback Ribs with Peach Glaze   62
Lemon Dill Salmon Patties with Pickly Peach Relish   64
Salmon Peach Bruschetta   66

Peachy Tomato Risotto with Shrimp 68

Chicken Peach Stir-Fry 70

Peach Tomato Chutney for Pork or Lamb Chops 72

Tangy Peach Barbecue Sauce 74

Desserts 75

Peach Schnappy Crème Brûlée 76

Sumptuous Peach Ice Cream 77

Creamy Peach Rice Pudding 78

Brandy Peach Cake 80

Blueberry Peach Frozen Smoothie Pops 81

Buttermilk Peach Cobbler 82

Peach Raspberry Fool and Nana's
    Shortbread Cookies 84

Cinnamon Peach Cream Puffs with
    Melba Sauce 86

Meringue Shells with Zesty Lemon Curd
    and Peach Strawberry Topping 88

Peach Raspberry Shortcake 90

Almond Sugar Cookie Cups with Creamy
    Peach Mousse 92

Lemon Peach Meringue Pie 94

Peach Upside-Down Cake with Rum Cream 96

Peaches and Cream Cheese Crusted Pie 98

Peaches Foster 100

Mixed-Fruit Crisp 102

Grilled Peaches with Amaretto Sauce 104

Index 105

About the Author 109

Preface

Peaches are many people's favorite fruit, and it's easy to understand why. Sweet and succulent, these creamy, fleshed globes send juices dribbling down the chin and douse the fingers with sticky nectar. Their intense sweet smell indicates ripeness and flavor, which are at their peak freshly picked at roadside stands in the heat of summer.

Peaches augment the shape, texture, and taste of any preparation, so it was an easy task choosing peaches as the main ingredient for this book. They lend themselves to a wealth of recipes even more so than the star of my last book, mushrooms. (Mushrooms fall short in the dessert category.)

When writing up a recipe, I always keep the home cook in mind. If the recipe is not easy to follow, who needs it? After honing my recipe-development skills in the test kitchens of *Food & Wine* magazine and *Woman's World*, I savored the idea of experimenting in my own kitchen, creating a wide range of recipes.

When I'm in my cooking domain, I jot down ideas, think up ingredients that work well together, and figure out whether certain combinations are right together. Seasonings and herbs are the pièce de résistance, which give the dish its final nod of approval.

In this book, peaches maintain their starring dessert role and also find new character depth in beverages, breakfast items, appetizers, entrées, soups, and salads, lending themselves to myriad preparations and creations. Their succulent nature perks up classic guacamole with chunky sweetness. They give a candylike element to tangy barbecue sauce and punctuate leeks and prosciutto in a side dish. Peach chive butter seeps in and downplays the heat of the meat in a spicy skirt steak recipe, and chopped fresh peaches pump up a pesto penne pasta dish.

Classic desserts such as peach melba and crème brûlée are served up with a peach twist from tradition. The melba can be made the authentic way by poaching the peaches, or by grilling peach halves, which increases their sugary intensity. Crème brûlée gets an added kick with a splash of peach schnapps permeating this silky custard.

Make your meals more sumptuous and inviting with these peach-enhanced recipes. Everyone's favorite fruit is now ripe for these inventive dishes.

There are a few people I would like to acknowledge for their parts in making this book a reality. First and foremost, I thank Kyle Weaver, editor at Stackpole Books, for giving me the opportunity to write my second cookbook. I am also grateful to Alan Wycheck, who did an excellent job of photographing every recipe. He went beyond the call of duty by sampling each peach concoction too. Thanks also to my sisters Penny Hannegan, Lisa Whitlock, and their families, for tasting some preliminary recipes and offering feedback. Unfortunately, those first attempts didn't make it into the book. And finally, I thank my family, Rick, Andrew, Ellen, Nikki, and Liza. They are taking a little peach hiatus after a peachy-keen and abundant year of fruit-filled dishes—although my mother-in-law, Janet W. Legro, never gets tired of peach-scented crème brûlée.

All About Peaches

t didn't take long for a passion for peaches to circle the globe. Discovered by the Chinese, these blushing beauties were first cultivated as far back as tenth century B.C. Today, peaches are a favored fruit in more than sixty countries around the world.

From China, peaches followed trade routes to the Middle East, Turkey, Russia, and Persia (today's Iran). Alexander the Great is said to have taken peaches from Persia to Greece; the Romans were later responsible for distributing peaches throughout Europe. The Romans are also credited with giving the peach its botanical name, *Prunus persica*, or Persian apple, erroneously suggesting that the peach originated in Persia. In France, the peach caught the eye and palate of the extravagant Sun King Louis XIV. French varieties of peaches took on feminine names, such as Belle de Chevreuse, Reine des Yergers, and Belle de Paris.

Arriving in the New World via French and Spanish explorer ships, peaches began growing along the East Coast and into Mexico as early as the sixteenth century. Peach trees were easy to grow and prolific, and Native Americans quickly spread them from the South to the North and eventually to the West Coast. American colonists also boosted the prevalence of the peach tree, because the tree bore fruit quickly and the pits were easy to transport. By the mid-eighteenth century, Thomas Jefferson had planted more than thirty-eight varieties of peaches, 160 trees, at his Monticello residence in Virginia.

Today the United States produces 20 percent of the world's peaches. The largest producer of peaches in the country is California, and the second-largest is South Carolina. At one point, the turn-of-the-century

Del Monte fruit cannery in San Francisco was the biggest in the world. The Cannery, as it's known today, is now a unique complex at Fisherman's Wharf featuring restaurants and shops. Peaches are the state fruit of Georgia, Alabama, and South Carolina.

Peaches are available from May to October in most areas of the United States. Throughout most of the winter, many supermarkets import them from Southern Hemisphere countries, and they are always readily available canned, dried, and frozen. Of course, the best peaches are the freshly picked ones sold in the summer at roadside stands. These are fragrant and so juicy that you'd better have a napkin ready to mop up your chin after taking a bite.

Peaches are members of the rose family *Rosaceae*. They are closely related to apricots, cherries, plums, almonds, and especially their kid sister, the nectarine. Nectarines may be used interchangeably with peaches in these recipes. They are a naturally occurring variety of peaches that was originally a mutant. They are very similar to peaches, except they lack the gene that gives peaches their fuzzy skin and are frequently

smaller. Peaches come in white and yellow varieties, with the skin ranging in color from pink-blushed creamy white skin to red-blushed yellow.

White peaches, which have a pinkish skin and white, creamy flesh, tend to be sweeter and less acidic than yellow peaches. Peento, or Pan Tao, peaches are flat or doughnut shaped. These varieties also are often sweeter than yellow peaches.

Hundreds of varieties of peaches can be found around the world today, but they fall into two basic categories: cling and freestone. In the cling peaches, the flesh clings to the pit. These peaches are often firmer textured than freestone. In the Northern Hemisphere, cling peaches are early to ripen and the first to be harvested, from May to August. They are widely used commercially for canning and freezing. In freestone peaches, the pit is loose and easily removed from the flesh. These peaches are good for eating out of hand, freezing, or cooking. It's easy to slice or dice them, and they retain their shape after the stone is removed. The fresh peaches you find at farmers' markets and in supermarket produce sections are typically freestone rather than cling.

Peaches make a very nutritious snack or addition to any meal. They are a good source of vitamins A and C and the minerals calcium, phosphorus, iron, and potassium. These fruits are low in calories, with about 35 calories in a small peach and 60 calories in a large one. They have no cholesterol or fat and are high in fiber and rich in antioxidants. Because they are processed within twenty-four hours of picking, canned and frozen peaches retain their nutritional value.

When choosing fresh preaches, the flesh should give slightly when pressed lightly with the fingers. Be careful not to press too hard, as these fruits bruise easily and you can create little fingertip dents. Look for peaches that have an intense, sweet smell and creamy yellow or pale golden skin, especially close to the stem. There should be no sign of green, brown, wrinkles, or bruises. Any green patches on the skin indicate that the peach was picked prematurely, and these fruits do not ripen well once picked. The degree of red blush does not determine ripeness, but depends on the variety of the peach. Peaches should be picked when they are just ripe: don't buy ones that are overly soft. To help ripen firm-textured peaches, keep them in a brown paper bag for a day or two.

It's best to store and eat peaches at room temperature as taste and texture deteriorate once refrigerated. Peaches will last one to three days on the counter at room temperature or up to five days in the crisper drawer in the refrigerator.

To store peaches for longer periods, sprinkle slices with lemon juice, and then freeze on a cookie sheet or plate until firm. Transfer slices to Ziploc bags and keep in the freezer. Slices will darken slightly, but they will still taste sweet and fresh in cooked and baked recipes or in smoothies.

Here are a few cooking hints: To remove the skin, dip peaches into boiling water for 30 seconds, then transfer to cold water with a slotted spoon. The skins will slip off easily. Sprinkle the flesh of cut peaches with lemon juice to prevent darkening. When determining the number of peaches you'll need for a recipe, keep in mind that 3 medium peaches equal about 1 pound or 2 cups sliced or $1^1/2$ cups puree.

Beverages

Peachy White Wine Sangria

On a hot, sunny afternoon next to the pool, there's nothing more lip-smacking delicious than a glass of this unique sangria.

750-milliliter bottle peach chardonnay or dry white wine
1/2 cup peach schnapps
2 peaches, pitted and thinly sliced
1/2 lemon, thinly sliced
1/2 lime, thinly sliced
grenadine syrup (optional)
maraschino cherries (for garnish)
mint sprigs (for garnish)

In large glass pitcher, combine first 5 ingredients. Chill at least 4 hours. Fill pitcher with ice and drizzle with a splash of grenadine syrup. Strain into glasses. Top each drink with a cherry and a mint sprig. You can also retrieve the peaches with a slotted spoon and add them to the glasses. Serves 4 to 6.

Peach Crantini

Summery and refreshing, this hot-weather drink takes the heat off. Peach nectar is available in the fruit juice section of most supermarkets. The white cran peach juice gives this drink its underlying burst of sweetness.

ice cubes
3 ounces peach vodka
3 ounces white cran peach
  juice
1 ounce peach nectar
1 fresh peach cut into 4 slices,
  peeled and pitted
fresh mint (for garnish)

In a martini shaker, add ice cubes, peach vodka, white cran peach juice, peach nectar, and peach slices. Shake vigorously and strain into individual martini glasses. Using tongs or a slotted spoon, pick out peach slices and add to martini glass with a garnish of mint. Makes 2 servings.

Sparkling Peach Lemonade

Serve ice-filled pitchers of this lemonade with a peach twist as a refreshing, hot-afternoon thirst quencher.

1^1/4 cups peach puree (about 4 large, fresh peaches)
1^1/3 cups lemon juice
^{3}/4 cup to 1 cup sugar or to taste
1 cup sparkling water or club soda
strawberry slices (for garnish)

To make peach puree, cut flesh from peaches close to pit. Add peach pieces to blender and puree until smooth. Using blender, stir in lemon juice and sugar. Pour into 8-ounce beverage glasses filled with ice and stir in sparkling water. Garnish with strawberry slices. Makes 6 servings.

Strawberry Peach Smoothie

Smoothies are simple, fast, and nutritious drinks. My kids love to whip up this recipe before heading off to school. Peaches may be used with the skin on or off.

> 1 cup coarsely chopped peaches
> 6-ounce container (about $^2/_3$ cup) peaches and cream yogurt
> $^1/_2$ cup coarsely chopped strawberries
> 1 cup ice

In blender, puree first 3 ingredients. Add ice and puree until smooth. Pour into glasses and serve immediately. Makes $2^1/_2$ cups.

Peach Bellini

A little dollop of peach puree slips a bit of sweet succulence into a glass of well-chilled champagne.

1 fresh juicy ripe peach,
   peeled, pit removed,
   coarsely chopped
1 teaspoon sugar or to taste,
   depending on sweetness
   of peach
1-liter bottle of dry
   champagne

In a food processor, puree peach and stir in sugar. Divide peach puree among 4 champagne flutes. Slowly pour in champagne. Drink immediately. Repeat as desired. Makes 4 bellinis.

Peach Sunrise

Like the dawning of a new day, this rosy layered drink is reminiscent of a tequila sunrise minus the alcohol.

> 4 ounces peach nectar
> 4 ounces limeade
> splash of grenadine syrup
> squeeze of fresh lemon
> mint leaves and fresh peach
>   slices (for garnish)

In a tall beverage glass, mix equal portions of peach nectar and limeade. Pour in a drizzle of grenadine syrup and a squeeze of lemon. Garnish the edge of the glass with mint leaves and a fresh peach slice. Serves 1.

Breakfast Treats

Cinnamon Peach Muffins

Change the color and texture of these fruity muffins by substituting 1/2 cup fresh or frozen blueberries for 1/2 cup of peaches.

12/3 cups flour
2 teaspoons baking powder
1 teaspoon cinnamon
1/4 teaspoon salt
1 egg
2/3 cup sugar
2/3 cup buttermilk
1 teaspoon vanilla
1/2 cup (1 stick) unsalted butter, melted
11/2 cups 1/2-inch diced peaches
2 tablespoons sugar

Preheat oven to 400 degrees. Line muffin tins with muffin papers. In medium bowl, combine flour, baking powder, cinnamon, and salt. In another medium bowl, whisk together egg, 2/3 cup sugar, buttermilk, and vanilla. Stir in melted butter and then flour mixture just until combined. Fold in peaches. Fill muffin cups two-thirds of the way up, and sprinkle tops with remaining 2 tablespoons sugar. Bake for 15 to 20 minutes, until toothpick inserted in center of muffins comes out clean. Let cool on rack. Serve warm or at room temperature. Makes 12 muffins.

Yogurt with Fresh Peaches and Nutty Granola

This homemade granola makes a tasty and nutritious breakfast sprinkled over a bowl of yogurt topped with fresh peaches. This simple recipe also makes a good base granola. You can add other items such as chocolate chips, toasted coconut, peanuts, or bits of pretzel to make a tasty snack or trail mix.

1 1/2 cups old-fashioned oats
1/2 cup sliced almonds
2 tablespoons brown sugar
1/4 teaspoon salt
3 tablespoons maple syrup
2 tablespoons vegetable oil
raisins, cranraisins, or other dried fruit (optional)
plain or vanilla yogurt
chopped fresh peaches

Preheat oven to 325 degrees. In medium bowl, use a fork to toss together oats, almonds, brown sugar, and salt. Toss in maple syrup and oil. Spread oat mixture across cookie sheet and bake, stirring occasionally, until deep golden brown, 25 to 30 minutes. Don't burn the nuts or they will be bitter. Let cool completely. If desired, toss in raisins or other dried fruits. Sprinkle a handful of granola over yogurt topped with peaches. Makes about 2 1/4 cups of granola.

Lemon Peach Crumb Cake

You can serve this tender, buttery crumb cake at breakfast or brunch.
It's also delicious served warm topped with vanilla ice cream as dessert.

2^1/$_2$ cups cake flour
2^1/$_2$ teaspoons baking powder
^{1}/$_2$ teaspoon baking soda
^{1}/$_2$ teaspoon salt
12 tablespoons (1^1/$_2$ sticks) unsalted butter,
   room temperature
1^1/$_2$ cups sugar
3 eggs
1 teaspoon lemon zest
1 cup plain yogurt
1^1/$_2$ cups diced fresh peaches
^{1}/$_2$ cup sliced or slivered almonds
Lemon Crumb Topping (recipe on opposite page)

Preheat oven to 350 degrees. Butter a 13 x 9 x 2-inch baking pan. Start by making the Lemon Crumb Topping, and put in refrigerator until ready to use. Then, in a medium bowl, sift together flour, baking powder, baking soda, and salt. In large mixing bowl, beat butter until creamy. Gradually add sugar, and beat until light and fluffy. Beat in eggs, one at a time, then beat in the lemon zest. Slowly beat in the flour mixture, alternating with the yogurt, in 3 batches, until well blended. Fold peaches into batter, and smooth into buttered pan. Crumble the topping evenly over the top, and sprinkle with almonds. Bake for 45 to 50 minutes, until golden brown and a toothpick inserted in the middle comes out clean. Makes 12 servings.

Note: If you use a food processor to dice the peaches, chop them finely, turning the machine on and off. Don't puree.

Lemon Crumb Topping

3/4 cup cake flour
1/2 cup sugar
1/2 teaspoon salt
1 teaspoon grated lemon zest
6 tablespoons (1 stick) unsalted butter, chilled
   and cut into small pieces

In a small bowl, combine flour, sugar, salt, and lemon zest. Add the butter, and cut in with a pastry blender or fingertips until mixture just begins to form small clumps. Refrigerate.

Baked Oatmeal with Peaches and Whipped Cream

The crumbly texture of the baked oatmeal is superbly accompanied by juicy fresh peaches and fluffy whipped cream. Don't be alarmed by the wet texture of the mixture before it's baked.

3 cups old-fashioned oats
1 cup brown sugar
2 teaspoons baking powder
1 teaspoon cinnamon
1 teaspoon salt
2 eggs
$1/2$ cup melted unsalted butter
$3/4$ cup milk
$1/2$ cup sour cream
1 teaspoon vanilla
fresh peach slices (for garnish)
sweetened whipped cream

Preheat oven to 350 degrees. Butter a 12 x 9 x $2^1/2$-inch baking dish. In large bowl, whisk together oats, brown sugar, baking powder, cinnamon, and salt. In medium bowl, whisk together eggs, butter, milk, sour cream, and vanilla. Stir egg mixture into oat mixture until combined. Spread evenly into prepared dish. (Mixture will be a little wet looking.) Bake for 35 to 40 minutes, until toothpick inserted in the center comes out clean. Let cool slightly, then cut into squares. Dollop each serving with whipped cream and spoon peaches over top. Makes 8 servings.

Fresh Fruit Kabobs

A stunning combination, this blend of fruit pairs well with dipping sauce kissed with peach schnapps or Grand Marnier.

>   1 large peach, peeled, pitted, and cut into 8 slices, then halved
>   1 kiwifruit, ends removed, peeled and cut lengthwise into 8
> $^1/_2$-inch slices
>   8 pineapple chunks, about 1 inch
>   8 strawberries, stems removed and large ones cut in half
>   8 wooden bamboo skewers
> $^1/_2$ cup plain yogurt
>   2 tablespoons powdered sugar
>   1 tablespoon peach schnapps or Grand Marnier

Skewer fruit onto 8 bamboo skewers, alternating peaches, kiwifruit, pineapple, and strawberries. In small bowl, stir together yogurt, powdered sugar, and peach schnapps or Grand Marnier. Scrape dipping sauce into serving bowl and serve with fruit kabobs. Makes 8 kabobs.

Blackberry Peach French Toast

Prepare this company-size, fruit-studded French toast the night before and bake in the morning.

12 cups 1-inch cubed sourdough or firm white bread
1¹/₂ cups diced fresh, frozen, or canned and drained peaches
1 pint fresh or frozen blackberries or blueberries
8-ounce package cream cheese, cut into small dice
8 eggs
1 cup milk
¹/₂ cup heavy cream
¹/₂ cup maple syrup
¹/₂ cup (1 stick) melted butter
¹/₄ teaspoon salt
1 teaspoon vanilla

Butter a 13 x 9-inch baking pan. Sprinkle bread cubes over the bottom, then scatter peaches, berries, and cream cheese evenly over top. In medium bowl, whisk together eggs, milk, heavy cream, maple syrup, butter, salt, and vanilla. Pour mixture over bread cubes. Cover with plastic wrap and refrigerate overnight (at least 8 hours). In the morning, preheat oven to 350 degrees. Bake French toast uncovered for 40 to 50 minutes, until custard has set. Serve with maple syrup or Amaretto Sauce (see page 104).

Lemon Pound Cake
with Fresh Fruit Salad

My grandmother Nana made the best lemon pound cake, but whenever I made her recipe, the end result never tasted as good. So I made up my own recipe. This version mimics Nana's lemon loaf in texture and flavor, but the ingredients differ a little. Cake flour, for instance, gives this light, lemony cake its fine crumb. It makes a fabulous breakfast served with Fresh Fruit Salad and whipped cream.

> 2 cups cake flour
> 2 teaspoons baking powder
> 1/4 teaspoon salt
> 1 cup (2 sticks) unsalted butter, room temperature
> 1 cup sugar
> 4 eggs
> 2 tablespoons lemon juice
> 2 teaspoons grated lemon zest
> 1 tablespoon heavy cream
> 1 tablespoon sugar
> Fresh Fruit Salad (recipe on opposite page)
> whipped cream

Preheat oven to 350 degrees. Butter and flour a 9^1/4 x 5^1/4 x 2^3/4-inch loaf pan. In medium bowl, sift together cake flour, baking powder, and salt. In large mixing bowl, beat butter until light and fluffy. Gradually beat in 1 cup sugar. Add eggs one at a time, beating well after each addition. Beat in lemon juice and zest. With the mixer on low speed, gradually add flour mixture until combined. Scrape the batter into the prepared pan and smooth the top evenly. Drizzle the heavy cream over the loaf, and sprinkle with 1 tablespoon sugar. Bake in the middle of the oven for 50 to 60 minutes, or until a toothpick inserted in the center comes out clean. Let cool on wire rack for 5 minutes. Unmold and slice. Top each slice with Fresh Fruit Salad and a dollop of whipped cream. Makes 6 servings.

Fresh Fruit Salad

    1 kiwifruit, peeled, quartered, and sliced $1/4$ inch thick
    1 cantaloupe, halved, seeded, and scooped with a melon baller
    3 fresh peaches, peeled and cut into bite-size pieces
    1 pint fresh strawberries, cleaned and sliced in half
    1 pint fresh blueberries
    2 tablespoons sugar
    $1^1/2$ tablespoons lemon juice

Combine all the fruit in medium glass bowl. Sprinkle with sugar and lemon juice, and toss gently. Cover with plastic wrap and refrigerate for at least 2 hours. Can be made the night before when serving for breakfast. Serve on top of the Lemon Pound Cake or on its own.

Cranberry Orange Scones with Orchard Peach Jam

The key to making good scones is to have cold hands when rubbing the butter into the flour, so the butter won't melt. If your hands are always warm, like mine, use a food processor to mix the ingredients. It's easier, too. These light, airy scones pair well with homemade Orchard Peach Jam.

2 cups all-purpose flour
$1/4$ cup sugar
1 teaspoon grated orange zest
2 teaspoons baking powder
$1/2$ teaspoon baking soda
$1/4$ teaspoon salt
6 tablespoons cold unsalted butter, cut into small dice
1 egg, slightly beaten
$3/4$ cup heavy cream
$1/3$ cup craisins (sweetened dried cranberries)
1 tablespoon sugar
Orchard Peach Jam (recipe on opposite page)

Preheat oven to 400 degrees. In food processor, add flour, $1/4$ cup sugar, orange zest, baking powder, baking soda, and salt. Pulse on and off until combined. Add butter and pulse until mixture resembles cornmeal and butter is incorporated. Pour mixture into medium bowl, and stir in egg, cream, and craisins. Press mixture into a ball. Then press into a $1^1/2$-inch-thick disk. Sprinkle circle with remaining 1 tablespoon sugar, and carefully cut into 8 triangles. Arrange triangles evenly apart on greased cookie sheet. Bake 15 minutes, or until golden brown. Transfer to wire rack and let cool. Serve with Orchard Peach Jam. Makes 8 scones.

Orchard Peach Jam

As with any jam recipe, don't mess with the quantities of fruit and sugar, or the recipe won't set. I have made the mistake of reducing the sugar and then ending up with watery jam. I chop the peaches finely in a food processor or blender.

4$^1/_2$ cups finely chopped peeled, fresh peaches
1 tablespoon lemon juice
1.75 ounces (1 box) fruit pectin
$^1/_2$ teaspoon butter
5 cups sugar

In large saucepan, bring peaches and lemon juice to a full rolling boil. Stir in pectin and butter, and bring again to a full rolling boil. Stir in sugar all at once, and return to a full rolling boil for 1 minute. Skim off any foam and ladle jam into sterilized jars. Place sterilized lids on jars and seal. Makes 6$^1/_2$ cups of jam.

Lemon Ginger Peach Marmalade
for Croissants or Biscuits

The hardest part of this recipe is finely chopping the crystallized ginger. It doesn't work to use the food processor, which just makes thick, stuck-together dice. A sharp knife is your best bet. This may seem like a ton of sugar, but you will need all of it or the marmalade won't set. This marmalade makes a fantastic breakfast condiment, especially atop croissants or biscuits.

> 7 cups finely chopped peaches
> 4 thin-skinned bitter oranges, such as Seville
> 3 tablespoons lemon juice
> $1/2$ cup water
> $8^{1}/2$ cups sugar
> $3/4$ cup crystallized ginger, finely chopped
> 1.75 ounces (1 box) fruit pectin

Place peaches in large saucepan. Cut and discard ends of oranges, then cut into wedges and remove seeds. Put in food processor and pulse until finely chopped. Then stir oranges, lemon juice, and water in with peaches. Bring mixture to a boil and simmer for 10 minutes. Stir in sugar and ginger, then bring back to a full boil. Boil gently for 10 minutes longer. Stir in pectin, bring to a boil, and simmer 10 minutes more, or until mixture will set. To test for a set, place 1 teaspoonful on a plate and chill. If the marmalade wrinkles, thickens slightly, and forms a thin skin when you push your finger across it, it will set. If it will not set, cook an additional 5 minutes and test again. Makes 6 pints.

Appetizers

Peach Bruschetta Topping

Serve this light and refreshing topping over black peppercorn goat cheese on oven-baked baguette slices. Alternatively, you can substitute feta cheese (4 ounces) into the peach mixture and serve on crackers.

   1 baguette, sliced diagonally into 1/2-inch slices
   olive oil
   garlic salt or 1/2 clove fresh garlic
   1 garden-fresh tomato, diced
   1 fresh peach, peeled, pitted, and cut into fine dice
   1 tablespoon chopped fresh basil
   1 teaspoon balsamic vinegar
   1 teaspoon olive oil
   4 ounces black peppercorn goat cheese

Preheat oven to 400 degrees. Place baguette slices on cookie sheet, drizzle with olive oil, and sprinkle lightly with garlic salt or rub 1/2 clove of fresh garlic across each slice of bread. Bake in oven until golden brown, 2 to 3 minutes per side, flipping slices over once. Let cool. In medium bowl, combine tomato, peach, basil, balsamic vinegar, and 1 teaspoon olive oil. Spread baguette slices with goat cheese, and top with peach mixture. Serves 4 to 6.

Sesame Ginger Chicken Skewers with Spicy Peach Chipotle Sauce

Sweet chicken pieces get a kick of heat from Spicy Peach Chipotle Sauce. Crank up the heat in the sauce by adding more chipotle chiles.

$1/4$ cup soy sauce
2 tablespoons brown sugar
1 tablespoon hoisin sauce
2 tablespoons lemon juice
1 teaspoon sesame oil
1 clove garlic, minced
1 teaspoon grated or minced fresh ginger
pinch crushed red pepper flakes
1 pound chicken breasts, cut into 1-inch pieces
metal or bamboo skewers
Spicy Peach Chipotle Sauce (recipe below)

In medium bowl, stir together first 8 ingredients. Add chicken and marinate in refrigerator for up to 2 hours. When ready to cook, preheat grill or broiler. Thread chicken onto skewers. If using wooden skewers, soak them in cold water for $1/2$ hour first. Grill or broil on greased baking dish or cookie sheet, turning often, until just opaque throughout, 6 to 8 minutes. Serve Spicy Peach Chipotle Sauce on the side. Serves 4.

Spicy Peach Chipotle Sauce

1 fresh peach, peeled, pitted, and coarsely chopped
2 canned chipotle chilies packed in adobo sauce
2 tablespoons peach nectar

Puree all ingredients in a blender. Scrape into a small bowl and serve with chicken skewers for dipping.

Shiitake Shrimp Peach Tostadas

These elegant fruit-laced tostadas are perfect for supper on smoking-hot summer evenings.

^{1}/$_4$ cup sour cream
2 tablespoons heavy cream
2 teaspoons lime juice, divided
^{1}/$_4$ teaspoon cumin
^{1}/$_2$ cup corn or peanut oil for frying tortillas, or more if needed
4 corn tortillas
1 pound large shrimp, peeled and deveined
1 teaspoon chili powder
2 tablespoons olive oil, divided
1 diced jalapeño, seeds removed
2^1/$_2$ cups sliced shiitake mushrooms, about 5 ounces
1 cup diced fresh peaches
^{1}/$_2$ cup sliced green onions
2 teaspoons chopped mint, cilantro, or parsley (for garnish)
salt and pepper to taste

In small bowl, mix together sour cream, heavy cream, 1 teaspoon lime juice, and cumin. Set aside. In large skillet, fry tortillas in oil over moderately high heat, flipping once, until golden brown and crispy (1 to 2 minutes). Set aside tortillas. Carefully pour out excess oil and wipe skillet with a paper towel. In small bowl, toss shrimp with remaining 1 teaspoon lime juice and chili powder. In skillet, heat 1 tablespoon olive oil over moderate heat. Stir in shrimp and cook 1 minute. Stir in jalapeño, mushrooms, peaches, and green onions. Cook until shrimp are pink and mushrooms and peaches are heated through, 2 to 3 minutes. Toss in chopped fresh herbs and season with salt and pepper. To serve, place fried tortilla on plate. Dollop sour cream sauce over tortilla and mound ^{1}/$_4$ of shrimp mixture in the center of each fried tortilla. Repeat with remaining 3 tortillas. Serves 4 as an appetizer or 2 as the main course.

Prosciutto-Wrapped Peaches

Peaches replace the melon slices in this classic starter. I like to serve 2 or 3 prosciutto-wrapped peaches as a preliminary to a light summer meal. Use a vegetable peeler to make the cheese shavings.

1 bunch watercress, washed and trimmed
4 fresh peaches, peeled, pitted, and quartered
8 thin slices of prosciutto, cut in half lengthwise
Raspberry Vinaigrette (see page 44)
shavings of fresh Romano or Parmesan cheese

Arrange a bed of watercress on serving platter. Wrap each slice of peach with prosciutto and place atop watercress. Sprinkle lightly with Raspberry Vinaigrette (see page 44). Sprinkle cheese shavings over all and serve. Makes 5 to 8 servings.

Peach Guacamole

Chunky peaches add an element of sweetness to traditional guacamole. Serve with tortilla chips or dollop over chicken fajitas.

2 avocados, pitted and scooped out from skin
1 ripe peach, pitted and finely chopped
2 tablespoons finely chopped red onion
1 small garlic clove, minced
1 tablespoon lemon juice
1 tablespoon chopped fresh cilantro leaves
salt and pepper

In medium bowl, mash avocados to a chunky pulp. Stir in remaining ingredients. Makes 1 1/4 cups.

Blackened Scallops with Fresh Peach Sauce and Balsamic Reduction

Heat and sweet come together in this striking appetizer. You may simplify this first course by omitting Peach Puree and Balsamic Reduction. Instead, serve fresh diced peaches and blackened scallops over a bed of lightly dressed arugula or mixed greens.

1 teaspoon paprika
1$^1/_2$ teaspoons garlic powder
$^1/_4$ teaspoon crushed red pepper flakes
1$^1/_2$ teaspoons brown sugar
$^1/_4$ teaspoon salt
6 sea scallops, about $^1/_2$ pound
1 tablespoon olive oil for sautéing
Peach Puree (recipe below)
Balsamic Reduction (recipe on opposite page)

In small bowl, using a fork or fingertips (to disperse brown sugar), combine paprika, garlic powder, brown sugar, crushed red pepper flakes, and salt. Dust scallops all over with this spice rub. In large heavy skillet, sauté scallops over moderately high heat until opaque throughout, about 1 to 2 minutes per side. Place on a platter and cover loosely with foil while you make the sauces. To serve, place a pool of Peach Puree on 2 individual plates. Place 3 scallops on top and drizzle with Balsamic Reduction. Serves 2.

Peach Puree

$^1/_3$ cup chopped fresh peaches
1 tablespoon olive oil
1 tablespoon white wine vinegar

Puree peaches, oil, and vinegar in a blender.

Balsamic Reduction

$^1/_2$ cup balsamic vinegar
1 teaspoon sugar
$^1/_8$ teaspoon salt

Place balsamic vinegar, sugar, and salt in small saucepan. Bring to a boil over moderately high heat, then reduce to a simmer. Simmer until mixture is reduced by half and thickened slightly, 2 to 3 minutes.

Summer-Ripe Salsa

Summer's peak tomatoes and peaches freshen up this light, very flavorful salsa, which is a refreshing appetizer served with tortilla chips. It's also a wonderful accompaniment dolloped over grilled pork tenderloin, chicken, or thick fillet of fish such as swordfish or tuna. Spoon on the salsa about 10 minutes before serving to allow the meat or fish to absorb the fruity juices.

2 tomatoes, peeled and seeded, or 1 pint cherry or grape tomatoes
1 peach, peeled and coarsely cut from pit
3 tablespoons chopped red onion
1 finely chopped jalapeño, seeds removed
2 tablespoons olive oil
1 tablespoon lime juice
1 tablespoon chopped fresh cilantro
1 small clove garlic, minced
1/4 teaspoon ground cumin
salt and pepper to taste

In food processor, chop tomatoes. Scrap into medium bowl. Add peach to processor and coarsely chop. Scrap into bowl with tomatoes. Stir in remaining ingredients. Makes 2 cups.

Soups, Salads, and Sides

Chilled Peach Soup

This soup makes a refreshing starter to a summer meal. A pinch of chopped fresh mint over each bowl pumps up both flavor and presentation.

4 peaches, peeled and sliced
1 tablespoon lemon juice
2 tablespoons sugar, or to taste
$^1/_4$ cup plain yogurt
$^1/_4$ cup heavy cream
$^1/_4$ teaspoon ground cinnamon
crushed gingersnaps (for garnish)

In a blender, puree the first 6 ingredients. Pour into medium bowl, cover with plastic wrap, and refrigerate until chilled. Pour into individual bowls and sprinkle with crushed gingersnaps. Makes 2 servings.

Luscious Crab Peach Salad

This colorful salad also looks terrific spilling out of a hollowed tomato half or served on spiraled avocado slices over a bed of leafy lettuce. Crab Peach Salad is best served the day it is made.

8 ounces (about 1 cup) lump or backfin crabmeat
$^1/_3$ cup diced grape tomatoes
1 fresh peach, peeled, pitted, and cut into small dice
2 green onions, minced
3 tablespoons chopped fresh basil
$^1/_4$ cup mayonnaise
1 tablespoon lemon juice
1 teaspoon honey dijon mustard
$^1/_4$ teaspoon salt
$^1/_8$ teaspoon freshly ground black pepper
2 tablespoons chopped fresh basil (for garnish)

In large bowl, toss together gently the crab, tomatoes, peach, green onions, and 3 tablespoons chopped basil. In small bowl, stir together mayonnaise, lemon juice, mustard, salt, and pepper. Toss dressing carefully into crab mixture. To serve, mound crab salad on a bed of mixed greens on a platter or individual plates. Sprinkle with 2 tablespoons chopped basil. Makes 4 servings.

Peach-Kissed Summer Squash Soup with Cilantro Cream

This summer vegetable soup gets its subtle sweet undertones from fresh peaches.

    2 tablespoons unsalted butter
    3 large shallots, chopped
    1 garlic clove, minced
    1 small yellow-fleshed potato, thinly sliced
    1 carrot, peeled and coarsely chopped
    2 small summer squash, sliced
    2 ripe fresh peaches, peeled
    2 cups chicken broth
    salt and white pepper to taste
    Cilantro Cream (recipe below)
    freshly chopped mint (for garnish)

In 2-quart saucepan, melt butter over medium heat. Stir in shallots and garlic. Cook until softened, about 2 minutes. Stir in potato, carrot, and squash. Slice peaches from their pit directly into saucepan to catch any juices. Stir in chicken broth. Partially cover and simmer for 18 to 20 minutes, until potato slices are tender. Let cool slightly. Working in batches, puree soup in blender or food processor until smooth. Return to pot and reheat. Add salt and pepper to taste. To serve, ladle soup into bowls, dollop with Cilantro Cream and shower with freshly chopped mint. Makes 4 servings.

Cilantro Cream

    3 tablespoons sour cream
    1 tablespoon heavy cream
    1 tablespoon chopped cilantro leaves, loosely packed
    1 teaspoon lemon juice
    pinch of salt

In small bowl, combine all 5 ingredients and stir until smooth.

Curried Peach Chicken Salad

Use an ice cream scoop to place portions of chicken salad over mixed greens, or spoon salad into pita pockets and add lettuce, tomato, and red onion.

$2^1/_2$ cups diced cooked chicken breast
$2/_3$ cup slivered almonds, toasted
$2/_3$ cup halved-lengthwise green seedless grapes
$1/_4$ cup thinly sliced scallions or snipped chives
$2/_3$ cup mayonnaise
$1/_4$ cup peach jam or preserves
$1^1/_2$ teaspoons curry powder
2 tablespoons chopped cilantro
1 teaspoon lemon juice
salt and pepper to taste

In medium bowl, combine chicken, almonds, grapes, and scallions or chives. In small bowl, stir together mayonnaise, peach jam, curry, cilantro, and lemon juice. Scrape into chicken mixture, and toss to combine. Season with salt and pepper. Makes 8 $1/_2$-cup servings.

Indian Spiced Lentils with Peaches

2$^1/_2$ cups chicken broth
$^3/_4$ cup lentils
1 teaspoon curry seasoning
8-ounce can peaches in heavy
    syrup or 1 fresh peach,
    diced, plus an additional
    $^1/_4$ cup chicken broth
$^1/_4$ cup golden raisins
$^1/_4$ cup finely chopped toasted
    pecans
2 tablespoons finely chopped
    green onions
1 tablespoon chopped fresh
    cilantro
salt and pepper to taste

In cast-iron or nonstick skillet, bring chicken broth to a boil. Stir in lentils, curry, and syrup from peaches. Cover and simmer until tender, about 50 to 55 minutes. Stir in peaches, raisins, pecans, green onions, and cilantro. Heat through. Season to taste.

Peach Salad with Raspberry Vinaigrette

Serve as a side salad or add grilled chicken or shrimp to make a light midsummer meal.

7 cups (10-ounce package) shredded mixed greens
1/4 cup thinly sliced red onion
1 very ripe, juicy peach, sliced
2 ounces (about 4 tablespoons) Montrachet
   or other goat cheese, crumbled
2 tablespoons toasted sliced almonds
Raspberry Vinaigrette (recipe below)

In large bowl, toss greens with desired amount of Raspberry Vinaigrette. Divide greens among 4 salad plates. Arrange slices of onions, peaches, and goat cheese over each portion. Sprinkle with toasted almonds. Makes 4 servings.

Raspberry Vinaigrette

This dressing can also be used to marinate chicken. Drizzle over 4 chicken breast halves before grilling. The dressing is used on prosciutto-wrapped peaches as well (see page 32). Raspberry vinaigrette is also available at the grocery store.

1 tablespoon fresh raspberry puree
1 teaspoon sugar
2 tablespoons balsamic vinegar
1/3 cup olive oil
salt and pepper to taste

To make the raspberry puree, press fresh raspberries through a sieve until you have the required amount. Discard seeds. In small bowl, whisk the puree together with the sugar and vinegar. Slowly whisk in olive oil. Adjust seasonings. Makes about 1/2 cup dressing or marinade.

Lemon Barley Salad with Peaches

This refreshing salad adds citrusy perkiness to grilled chicken or pork. Make this recipe a day or two in advance in order for the ingredients to mellow and marry into a delightful bouquet.

$2^1/_3$ cups water
$^1/_2$ teaspoon salt
$^3/_4$ cup barley
1 red bell pepper, cut into small dice
1 fresh peach, peeled, sliced, and cut into small dice
2 green onions, finely chopped
1 jalapeño, cut into small dice
$^1/_3$ cup chopped fresh parsley leaves
1 tablespoon chopped fresh mint
$^1/_3$ cup buttermilk
3 tablespoons olive oil
3 tablespoons lemon juice
salt and pepper to taste

In medium saucepan, bring water and $^1/_2$ teaspoon salt to a boil. Stir in barley, cover, and simmer until tender and liquid is absorbed, about 45 to 50 minutes. In large bowl, toss together barley, red bell pepper, diced peach, green onions, jalapeño, and chopped herbs. In small bowl, whisk together buttermilk, olive oil, and lemon juice. Pour over barley mixture. Season with salt and pepper. Cover and refrigerate until ready to serve, or serve at room temperature. Makes 4 to 6 servings.

Note: You can substitute one 8-ounce can peaches, drained and cut into small dice.

Creamy Leeks and Peaches

This side dish makes a lovely accompaniment to fish or chicken. Pancetta is cured Italian bacon that is slightly salty. You can use hickory-smoked bacon too.

3 tablespoons unsalted butter
3 medium leeks, white and some of green, washed thoroughly, then sliced into 1/4-inch rounds
1/3 cup chicken broth
1/4 cup heavy cream
1 cup fresh, canned, or frozen peaches, diced
1/2 cup cooked and crumbled pancetta
parmesan or romano cheese, grated
chervil leaves or freshly chopped parsley
salt and pepper to taste

In large skillet, melt the butter over moderate heat. Stir in leeks, turn heat to low, and cook until almost tender, about 10 minutes. Stir in chicken broth and cream and bring to a boil. Simmer until liquid is reduced by half, 3 to 5 minutes. Add peaches and heat through. Sprinkle with pancetta, cheese, chervil or parsley, salt, and pepper. Serve warm. Makes 2 to 4 servings.

Pine Nut Peach Couscous

Quick and easy, couscous makes a great bed on which to serve vegetables and grilled meats.

1/4 cup pine nuts
2 tablespoons butter
1 clove garlic, minced
3 green onions, sliced thinly
1 cup chopped crimini or
  white mushrooms
1 1/2 cups chicken broth
1/2 teaspoon cinnamon
1/4 teaspoon cumin

1/2 teaspoon salt
1/8 teaspoon freshly ground
  black pepper
1 cup couscous
1/2 cup diced peaches
2 tablespoons chopped fresh
  parsley
squeeze of lemon juice
salt and pepper to taste

In a 10-inch dry skillet, cook pine nuts over moderate heat until browned, 1–2 minutes. Scrape into a small bowl and set aside. In same skillet, melt butter over moderate heat. Stir in garlic, green onions, and mushrooms and cook until softened, about 2 minutes. Stir in chicken broth, cinnamon, cumin, and salt, and bring to a full boil. Stir in couscous. Remove from heat, cover, and let sit 5 minutes. Fluff couscous with fork, and then stir in peaches, reserved pine nuts, parsley, and lemon juice. Add salt and pepper to taste. Makes 4 servings.

Entrées

Moroccan Peach Lamb Tagine

Make couscous or rice to go along with this stewy, peach-sweetened lamb dish. As an easier alternative, you can brown the meat and cook the vegetables in a skillet, then put meat, vegetables, wine, tomatoes, and broth in a Crock-Pot and cook on low heat for about 4 hours, until meat is tender. Stir in peaches, mint, and lemon at the end of cooking. Sliced zucchini and summer squash may be used in place of or along with carrots.

2 tablespoons flour
1 tablespoon smoked paprika
1/2 teaspoon salt
1/4 teaspoon freshly ground black pepper
1 pound lamb shoulder or beef stew meat cut into 1-inch pieces
    (stew meat)
2 tablespoons olive oil
2 tablespoons butter
1 small onion, chopped
2 garlic cloves, minced
1/2 cup red wine
1/2 pound (about 2 cups) baby carrots, peeled
1-pound, 12-ounce (28-ounce) can diced tomatoes (or 21/2 cups
    fresh tomatoes, chopped, peeled, and seeded, plus 1 cup
    tomato juice)
1 cup chicken or beef broth or water
1 cup fresh, frozen, or canned peaches, chopped
1 tablespoon chopped fresh mint
1 teaspoon lemon zest

In medium bowl, combine flour, paprika, salt, and pepper. Add lamb cubes and toss to coat completely. In large Dutch oven or saucepan, heat olive oil over moderately high heat. Add lamb and brown all over, about 5 minutes. Transfer meat to a bowl and set aside. Over moderate heat, melt butter in same saucepan. Add onion and garlic. Cook until onions are softened, about 6 minutes. Stir in red wine and let reduce for 1 minute. Stir in reserved lamb, carrots, tomatoes, and broth or water. Bring mixture to a boil, reduce heat, cover, and simmer until meat is fork-tender, about 11/2 to 2 hours. (The stew can be made 2 days ahead up to this point; reheat over low heat.) Stir in peaches, mint, and lemon zest. Heat through and serve. Serves 4 to 6.

Nut-Crusted Mahimahi
with Black Bean Fruit Salsa

Panko breadcrumbs are often found in the Asian section of the supermarket. I prefer these Japanese crumbs because of their fine, light texture. You can also make this recipe with red snapper fillets.

1/3 cup panko breadcrumbs
1/3 cup finely chopped pecans
2 tablespoons finely chopped scallions
1/2 teaspoon seafood seasoning
1/8 teaspoon pepper
1 egg, slightly beaten
4 mahimahi fillets, about 1 1/2 to 2 pounds
4 tablespoons melted butter
Black Bean Fruit Salsa (recipe on opposite page)

Preheat oven to 450 degrees. Place oven rack on top third of oven. In a medium bowl, mix together the first 5 ingredients. Place fillets on lightly greased cookie sheet. Brush one side of each fillet with egg, then pat on bread topping and drizzle each fillet with melted butter. Bake for 10 to 12 minutes, until opaque throughout. Cooking time should be about 10 minutes per inch of fillet.

Black Bean Fruit Salsa

This refreshing salsa can also be served as an appetizer with tortilla chips.

1¹/₂ cups (15.5-ounce can) black beans, drained and rinsed
1¹/₄ cups fresh or frozen corn kernels
8-ounce can crushed pineapple with juice
1 jalapeño, stemmed and seeded and cut into small dice
1 peach, sliced and cut into small dice
2 tablespoons chopped fresh cilantro leaves
2 tablespoons lemon juice
¹/₄ cup olive oil
pinch of cayenne
1 teaspoon sugar
salt and pepper to taste

In medium bowl, toss together first 6 ingredients. In small bowl, whisk together lemon juice, olive oil, cayenne, and sugar. Stir into black bean mixture. Season with salt and pepper. Serve at room temperature or chilled. Makes 4 cups.

Mustard-Thyme Chicken Thighs

Chicken thighs get a double dose of peaches. Fresh peach slices accentuate poultry pieces, while peach preserves give fruitiness to the sauce.

6 boneless, skinless chicken thighs, $1^1/2$ to 2 pounds, butterflied
$1/4$ cup honey mustard
$1^1/2$ teaspoons fresh thyme leaves or $1/2$ teaspoon dried
$1/4$ teaspoon salt
$1/8$ teaspoon pepper
2 tablespoons butter, divided
2 peaches, pitted and sliced into $1/4$-inch slices
1 tablespoon olive oil
1 large shallot, minced
1 garlic clove, minced
1 tablespoon cider vinegar
$1/2$ cup peach preserves
$1/4$ cup heavy cream
1 tablespoon chopped fresh parsley

Place chicken on large platter. Swipe mustard evenly over chicken thighs and sprinkle with thyme, salt, and pepper. Cover loosely and set aside. In a large nonstick skillet, heat 1 tablespoon butter over moderate high heat. Add peach slices and cook, tossing until softened and slightly golden, about 3 to 4 minutes. Transfer peach slices to a bowl and cover loosely with foil. Add olive oil to the skillet and heat over moderate high heat. Add chicken thighs and brown evenly on both sides, about 2 minutes. Cover and cook over moderate heat for 10 to 15 minutes, turning once, until chicken is opaque throughout. Transfer chicken to a platter and cover loosely with foil. In same skillet, melt remaining 1 tablespoon butter over high heat. Stir in shallot and garlic and cook until softened, about 1 minute. Stir in vinegar, peach preserves, and cream, and cook until slightly thickened, 1 to 2 minutes. Arrange chicken on a platter with peaches. Spoon sauce over chicken and peaches, sprinkle with parsley, and serve. For a more refined look to the sauce, strain out the bits of shallot and garlic before spooning it over the chicken.

Smoke-Rubbed Skirt Steak with Peach Chive Butter and Roasted Rosemary Potatoes

Skirt steak is becoming more and more popular, especially as a fajita component. This cut of meat is quite tender and juicy when marinated and grilled quickly. Flank steak may be substituted for the skirt steak. Peach Chive Butter provides added succulence as it seeps into the steak. You can use any leftover butter to season rice or couscous.

> 2 tablespoons Montreal seasoning
> 2 teaspoons smoked paprika
> 1 teaspoon garlic powder
> 1 1/2 pounds skirt steak
> 2 tablespoons olive oil
> Peach Chive Butter (recipe below)
> Roasted Rosemary Potatoes (recipe on opposite page)

Make Peach Chive Butter ahead of time and freeze until ready to use so that butter will hold its shape upon slicing. When ready to cook steak, preheat grill. In small bowl, combine Montreal seasoning, paprika, and garlic powder. Place skirt steak in a shallow pan, and sprinkle all over with seasoning mixture and olive oil. Grill steak 2 to 3 minutes per side for medium rare. Cut 1/8-inch rounds from frozen or semifrozen log of Peach Chive Butter, and place all over the top of the steak. Cover meat loosely with foil, and allow to rest for 10 minutes. Slice meat and serve with Roasted Rosemary Potatoes. This recipe serves 2 to 4.

Peach Chive Butter

> 4 tablespoons softened unsalted butter
> 2 tablespoons peach jam or preserves
> 1 teaspoon chopped fresh chives (or 1/2 teaspoon dried)
> 1/4 teaspoon salt

In small bowl, stir together butter, peach jam, chives, and salt. Scoop onto a square of waxed paper or plastic wrap, and squish into a log shape. Freeze.

Roasted Rosemary Potatoes

8 new potatoes, cut into $1/2$-inch pieces
2 teaspoons freshly chopped rosemary (or 1 teaspoon dried)
1 teaspoon garlic salt
freshly ground black pepper
2 tablespoons olive oil

Preheat oven to 400 degrees. Spray a 9 x 13-inch baking pan with vegetable oil. Add potatoes to prepared pan and toss with remaining ingredients. Bake for 40 to 45 minutes, until potatoes are tender and golden brown. Serves 4 to 6.

Pesto Penne Pasta with Peaches and Grilled Summer Vegetables

This recipe calls for two types of grilled squash. You can be creative and add other fresh or grilled vegetables, such as eggplant, broccoli, peas, or garden-ripe peppers. As a shortcut, you can use store-bought pesto instead of making your own.

1 cup basil leaves, loosely packed
$1/3$ cup parsley or cilantro leaves, loosely packed
$1/2$ cup grated Parmesan cheese
6 tablespoons olive oil
$1/2$ teaspoon salt
$1/2$ pound penne pasta
1 zucchini, sliced lengthwise
1 summer squash, sliced lengthwise
2 tablespoons olive oil
1 large fresh peach, peeled, pitted, and chopped
1 large tomato, seeded and diced
$1/2$ cup toasted pine nuts

Preheat grill or broiler. To make pesto, in blender or food processor, pulse together basil, parsley or cilantro, Parmesan cheese, 6 tablespoons olive oil, and salt. Set aside. In large pot of boiling salted water, cook pasta until al dente. Drain well, transfer to large bowl, and toss with pesto mixture. Brush squash with 2 tablespoons olive oil. Grill or broil about 2 minutes per side, turning once, until squash slices are lightly grilled. Let cool slightly, then slice crosswise into $1/4$-inch slices. Toss into pasta with peach, tomato, and pine nuts. Season to taste. Serves 6 to 8.

Spicy Pork Babyback Ribs with Peach Glaze

These ribs are easy to make and finger-licking delicious smothered with a spicy and tangy peach glaze. This recipe is ideal in the winter, when the lengthy cooking time of the ribs allows the smell to permeate the house. In summer, slow cook ribs on the grill.

3 tablespoons smoky mesquite seasoning, St. Louis style rib rub, or chili powder
1 tablespoon light brown sugar
2 teaspoons garlic powder
$1/4$ teaspoon cumin
$1/4$ teaspoon cayenne
$1/4$ teaspoon salt
$1/8$ teaspoon pepper
2 racks pork babyback ribs, $2^1/4$ to $2^1/2$ pounds each, cut racks in half
$1/2$ cup peach jam or preserves
$1^1/2$ tablespoons orange juice
$1/4$ teaspoon dried thyme leaves

Preheat oven to 350 degrees. In small bowl, combine first 7 ingredients. Sprinkle the ribs all over with the spice mixture. Stack and wrap ribs in a double thickness of foil, and place on a shallow roasting pan. Bake in the oven until fork-tender, about $1^1/2$ to 2 hours. Next, preheat broiler. Open up foil and lay both sets of racks of ribs side by side on the roasting pan, or if they don't fit laid out, use a cookie sheet. In small bowl, stir together peach jam, orange juice, and thyme. Spoon glaze over the top of each rack of ribs. Broil ribs on the top shelf of the oven 3 to 4 inches from the heat source, about 1 to 2 minutes, until glaze is hot and golden. Makes 8 servings.

Lemon Dill Salmon Patties with Pickly Peach Relish

These delicious patties are bound together using mashed potatoes rather than breadcrumbs or egg. This recipe is a great way to use up leftover grilled or baked salmon fillets. Patties will freeze well too; just slip them into Ziploc freezer bags.

1 small russet potato
$1/4$ cup plain yogurt
3 tablespoons mayonnaise
1 tablespoon lemon juice
1 teaspoon freshly chopped dill (or $1/2$ teaspoon dried)
2 tablespoons minced onion or green onion
$1/4$ teaspoon salt
$1/8$ teaspoon freshly ground black pepper
$1/2$ pound salmon fillet, cooked and flaked (about $1 1/4$ cups)
$1/2$ cup panko or regular breadcrumbs
1 tablespoon butter
1 tablespoon extra-virgin olive oil

Cook potato in microwave on high until tender, about 4 to 5 minutes. Cool slightly, peel, and mash with a fork to make about $1/2$ cup mashed potato. In medium bowl, stir together yogurt, mayonnaise, lemon juice, dill, onion, salt, and pepper. Stir in mashed potato and carefully toss in salmon flakes. Using a $1/3$ cup measuring cup, measure 4 rounded mounds and form into patties. Coat patties all over with the breadcrumbs. In large nonstick skillet, heat butter and olive oil over moderate heat. Cook salmon cakes until golden brown, about 2 to 3 minutes per side. Dollop with Pickly Peach Relish and serve with or without a bun. Makes 4 patties.

Pickly Peach Relish

This relish can be made up to 2 days in advance.

3 tablespoons mayonnaise
1 tablespoon hot dog relish or other pickle-based relish
1 tablespoon peach preserves or jam

In small bowl, mix together mayonnaise, relish, and preserves.

Salmon Peach Bruschetta

A classic bruschetta mixture takes on a sweet bite when permeated with diced peaches. Fresh, canned, or frozen peaches may be used in this recipe. For smaller appetites, cut down on the size of salmon per person.

    2 tablespoons olive oil
    2 large shallots, minced
    2 garlic cloves, minced
    6 plum tomatoes (about 1^1/2 pounds), diced
    2 peaches, peeled, pitted, and diced
    ^{1}/4 cup pitted Kalamata olives
    2 tablespoons capers, drained
    1 tablespoon lemon juice
    2 tablespoons chopped fresh basil
    salt and freshly ground black pepper to taste
    4 salmon fillets (about ^{1}/2 pound each)
    olive oil

Preheat grill or broiler. In large skillet, heat 2 tablespoons olive oil over moderate heat. Stir in shallots and garlic, and cook until softened, about 2 to 3 minutes. Stir in tomatoes, peaches, olives, and capers, and cook until liquid is reduced slightly, about 5 minutes. Stir in lemon juice and basil. Brush additional olive oil over fish fillets, and season with salt and pepper. Grill or broil about 3 inches from heat source, 3 to 5 minutes per side, until just opaque throughout. Arrange bruschetta on 4 plates and top with a fish fillet. Serves 4.

Peachy Tomato Risotto with Shrimp

Serve this colorful risotto with crusty bread and a lightly dressed salad.

4 cups homemade or canned chicken or vegetable broth,
  or more if needed
1 pound shrimp, peeled and deveined
1 tablespoon unsalted butter
3 medium tomatoes, peeled, seeded, and chopped
1 garlic clove, minced
2 tablespoons olive oil
1 small onion, finely chopped
$3/4$ cup Arborio rice
$1/4$ cup white wine
1 ripe peach, peeled and cut into nickel-size dice
$1/2$ cup chopped basil leaves, loosely packed
salt and freshly ground pepper to taste
grated Parmesan, Romano, or Asiago cheese

In medium saucepan, bring broth to a boil over moderately high heat. Add shrimp and cook until pink throughout, 1 to 2 minutes. Turn off heat and use a slotted spoon to remove shrimp to medium bowl. Strain and reserve warm liquid. In large nonstick skillet, melt butter over moderately high heat. Add tomatoes and garlic and cook, stirring, until liquid is evaporated, 3 to 5 minutes. Scrape tomato mixture into bowl with shrimp. Wipe skillet with paper towel. In same skillet, heat oil over moderate heat. Stir in onion and cook until softened, about 5 minutes. Stir in rice and cook until transparent, about 3 minutes. Stir in wine and cook until absorbed. Stir in reserved warm cooking liquid, $1/2$ cup at a time, until liquid is absorbed and rice is tender, 18 to 22 minutes. Rice should be tender to the bite; if not, add more chicken broth. Add reserved shrimp, tomatoes, diced peaches, and chopped basil and cook until heated through, 1 to 2 minutes. Season with salt and pepper. Spoon into big bowls and sprinkle with grated cheese. Serves 3 to 4.

Chicken Peach Stir-Fry

This attractive stir-fry is easy to assemble once chicken and vegetables are cut to size.

2 garlic cloves, minced
1 teaspoon freshly grated ginger
1 teaspoon sugar
2 tablespoons soy sauce
1 tablespoon sesame oil
1/4 teaspoon crushed red pepper flakes
4 boneless, skinless chicken breasts (about 11/2 pounds),
  thinly sliced into 2-inch pieces
2 tablespoons olive oil
1 red bell pepper, thinly sliced into 2-inch pieces
1 bunch asparagus, ends trimmed, then cut diagonally into
  2-inch pieces
1 peach, pitted and thinly sliced
2 green onions, sliced thinly
11/2 cups chicken broth
1 tablespoon cornstarch
1 tablespoon water
1 tablespoon chopped fresh cilantro

In medium bowl, combine garlic, ginger, sugar, soy sauce, sesame oil, and pepper flakes. Add chicken and marinate for 2 hours.

In large nonstick skillet, heat olive oil over moderately high heat. Add bell pepper, asparagus, peach slices, and green onions, and cook until peaches are soft and veggies are crisp-tender, about 3 to 5 minutes. Transfer mixture to medium bowl. Discard marinade and add chicken to pan. Cook chicken strips until almost opaque throughout, 2 to 3 minutes. Remove chicken and add to bowl with vegetables. Add chicken broth to pan and reduce for 2 minutes, scraping up any brown bits in the pan. Dissolve cornstarch in water. Stir dissolved cornstarch into chicken broth. Bring liquid to a boil, and boil until slightly thickened. Stir in reserved chicken, peach slices, vegetables, and cilantro. Serve immediately over steamed rice. Serves 4 to 6.

Peach Tomato Chutney
for Pork or Lamb Chops

Serve this spiced-up chutney with pork or stir in chopped, fresh mint leaves and dollop over grilled lamb chops.

2 tablespoons olive oil
$1/2$ cup chopped onion (about 1 small onion)
1 garlic clove, minced
$1/2$ cup chopped fresh peaches
1 medium tomato, peeled, seeded, and coarsely chopped
$1/3$ cup brown sugar
1 teaspoon chili powder
$1/2$ teaspoon mustard seed
$1/4$ teaspoon ground cumin
$1/4$ teaspoon ground cinnamon
2 tablespoons cider vinegar
2 tablespoons golden raisins (optional)

In skillet, heat olive oil over moderately high. Stir in onions and garlic. Cook, stirring, until onions are tender, 3 to 4 minutes. Stir in peaches, tomato, brown sugar, chili powder, mustard seed, cumin, cinnamon, and vinegar. Stir in raisins if desired. Continue to cook until juices thicken, about 6 minutes. Transfer to food processor and process until finely chopped but not pureed, turning on and off. Scrape into small bowl and dollop onto grilled pork or lamb chops. Makes 1 cup.

Tangy Peach Barbecue Sauce

This sauce goes particularly well with poultry. Baste poultry pieces with sauce before grilling or roasting in oven. Reserve some sauce to pass around.

> 1 tablespoon butter
> 1/2 cup chopped onion
> 2 garlic cloves, minced
> 1 1/2 cups chopped fresh peaches
> 1/4 cup ketchup
> 2 tablespoons dark brown sugar
> 1 tablespoon red wine vinegar
> 1 teaspoon Worcestershire sauce
> 2 teaspoons peach schnapps (optional)

In medium skillet, melt butter over medium heat. Stir in onion and garlic, and cook until softened, about 5 minutes. Stir in peaches, ketchup, brown sugar, vinegar, and Worcestershire sauce. Stir in schnapps if desired. Cook until thickened, about 5 minutes. Puree in blender until smooth. Makes 1 1/3 cups sauce.

Desserts

Peach Schnappy Crème Brûlée

Peach schnapps adds just the right amount of kick to this rich and deca-dent dessert, which is both impressive and easy to make. The key is not to let the water bath come to a boil. Add ice cubes to the water if necessary. I heat the cream in the microwave to get it hot.

5 egg yolks
^{1}/$_3$ cup sugar
2^1/$_4$ cups hot heavy cream
1^1/$_2$ tablespoons peach schnapps
3 teaspoons sugar

Preheat oven to 325 degrees. In medium bowl, whisk together egg yolks and ^{1}/$_3$ cup sugar. Stir in heavy cream and peach schnapps. Pour mixture into six ^{1}/$_2$-cup ramekins, and set in a 13 x 9 x 2-inch pan. Fill pan halfway up ramekins with water and place in middle of oven. Bake until custards are set, 50 minutes to 1 hour. Remove ramekins from water bath and refrigerate until chilled. The crème brûlée can be made a day in advance up to this point. Next, pre-heat broiler. Sprinkle ^{1}/$_2$ teaspoon sugar over the top of each ramekin. Place ramekins on top rack in oven and broil until sugar has caramel-ized, 1 to 2 minutes. Serve. Makes 6 servings.

Sumptuous Peach Ice Cream

Silky vanilla custard is the perfect complement to fresh peaches.

2 cups heavy cream
1 cup milk
1 cup sugar
pinch of salt
4 egg yolks
2 cups finely chopped fresh peaches
1 teaspoon vanilla

In microwavable bowl, heat cream and milk until hot. In medium saucepan, whisk together sugar, salt, and egg yolks. Whisk in hot liquid. Place saucepan over moderately high heat and cook, stirring, until bubbles disappear from custard surface and mixture coats the back of the spoon, about 8 to 10 minutes. Remove from heat and pour mixture into a bowl and chill. Stir in peaches and vanilla. Pour mixture into ice cream maker and follow manufacturer's instructions. Makes 5 cups.

Creamy Peach Rice Pudding

Made on the stove, this quick and easy pudding won't heat up the kitchen. I love the subtle sweetness of the peaches combined with the crunchy texture of the pistachios.

1 1/2 cups water
1/2 cup milk
1 cup medium-grain rice
1/2 teaspoon salt
pinch of nutmeg
1 cup heavy cream
1/3 cup sugar
1 cup diced fresh peaches
1/2 teaspoon vanilla
1/4 cup chopped pistachio nuts

In medium saucepan, bring water and milk to a boil. Stir in rice, salt, and nutmeg. Cover and cook until liquid is absorbed, 18 to 20 minutes. Uncover and stir in heavy cream and sugar. Bring to a boil and simmer, stirring, until most of the liquid has been absorbed and sugar is dissolved, about 5 minutes. Remove from heat and stir in peaches and vanilla. Spoon pudding into custard cups. Sprinkle with pistachio nuts just before serving. Serve warm, room temperature, or chilled. Makes 6 to 8 servings, about 4 cups pudding.

Brandy Peach Cake

This dessert smells as good as it tastes. Its cinnamony sweet aroma permeates the whole house. In the winter, make this cake using frozen peach slices cut into 1/2-inch dice.

3 cups all-purpose flour
2 teaspoons cinnamon
1 teaspoon ground ginger
1 teaspoon baking soda
1/2 teaspoon salt
1 cup (2 sticks) unsalted butter, room temperature
2 cups firmly packed dark brown sugar
4 eggs
1 teaspoon vanilla extract
3 tablespoons brandy or cognac
1/2 cup milk
2 1/2 cups fresh peaches, peeled, sliced, and cut into 1/2-inch dice
1 tablespoon confectioner's sugar

Preheat oven to 350 degrees. Butter and flour a 12-cup Bundt or tube pan. In medium bowl, whisk together flour, cinnamon, ginger, baking soda, and salt. In large mixing bowl, beat butter until light and creamy. Beat in brown sugar and eggs, one at a time. Beat in vanilla and brandy. On slow speed, beat in flour mixture, alternating with milk, in 3 batches. Fold in peaches and scrape mixture into prepared pan. Bake in middle of oven for 60 to 70 minutes, until a toothpick inserted in center of cake comes out clean. Let cool 10 minutes, then invert onto wire rack. After completely cool, sprinkle with confectioner's sugar.

Blueberry Peach Frozen Smoothie Pops

With their taste and texture, these pops resemble frozen smoothies. They're ideal substitutes to pricey store-bought frozen treats. Mix and match different fruits to create your favorite flavor.

1²/3 cups diced fresh, frozen, or canned peaches
¹/2 cup fresh or frozen blueberries
¹/3 cup sugar
1 teaspoon lemon juice

In a blender, puree all ingredients. Pour into eight ¹/4-cup molds. Freeze until firm. To unmold, run under hot water until pops are loosened. Makes 8.

Buttermilk Peach Cobbler

A subtle vanilla flavor permeates the moist cakey topping of this warm and homey cobbler. It's a good idea to place a piece of foil under the cobbler while cooking. Occasionally, juice from the peaches bubbles out from under the cobbler lid.

6 cups peach slices
$1/3$ cup sugar
$1^1/2$ teaspoons vanilla
$1/4$ teaspoon nutmeg
1 tablespoon flour
1 tablespoon softened butter
1 cup flour
1 teaspoon baking powder
$1/2$ teaspoon baking soda
pinch of salt
$2/3$ cup sugar
2 eggs
$1/2$ cup buttermilk
4 tablespoons melted butter

Preheat oven to 350 degrees. Butter a $10^1/2$-inch cast-iron skillet. In large bowl, toss together peach slices, $1/3$ cup sugar, 1 teaspoon vanilla, nutmeg, and 1 tablespoon flour. Scrape peach mixture into buttered skillet and dot with softened butter. Bake peaches until heated through, about 25 minutes. Meanwhile, in large bowl, whisk together 1 cup flour, baking powder, baking soda, salt, and $2/3$ cup sugar. In medium bowl, whisk together eggs, buttermilk, and melted butter. Add $1/2$ teaspoon vanilla. Stir buttermilk mixture into flour mixture just until combined. Pour evenly over hot peaches. Return skillet to oven until topping is golden brown and firm to the touch, 20 to 25 minutes. Serve warm with ice cream or whipped cream. Makes 6 servings.

Peach Raspberry Fool and Nana's Shortbread Cookies

You can substitute store-bought whipped cream for the heavy cream in the Fool; omit confectioner's sugar and stir in Grand Marnier. My grandmother used to bake the shortbread cookies every year when she came to visit at Christmastime. Nana brought this recipe from her hometown in Scotland.

4 peaches, sliced and cut into small dice
1 cup fresh raspberries, about 6 ounces (1/2 pint)
1 tablespoon sugar
1 tablespoon lemon juice
1 cup heavy cream
2 tablespoons confectioner's sugar
1 tablespoon Grand Marnier
whipped cream
Grated orange or lemon zest
Mint sprigs (optional)

In medium bowl, toss together peaches, raspberries, sugar, and lemon juice. Cover and set aside. In mixing bowl, beat cream, confectioner's sugar, and Grand Marnier until stiff peaks form. Divide fruit mixture among 6 glasses. Dollop with whipped cream. Grate orange or lemon zest over the top of the cream and pin with a mint sprig. Serves 6.

Shortbread Cookies

2 cups flour
1/2 cup brown sugar
1 cup (2 sticks) cold, unsalted butter, cut into small dice
pinch of salt
3 tablespoons granulated sugar

Preheat oven to 350 degrees. Grease two 9-inch round cake pans. In food processor, pulsing on and off, combine flour, brown sugar, butter, and salt until mixture begins to clump together. Divide shortbread dough into prepared cake pans. Press down evenly to smooth top. Using a knife, score each pan of shortbread into 8 even triangles. Sprinkle tops with granulated sugar. Bake 15 to 20 minutes, until lightly golden. Cut along scored markings while still warm. Prick decoratively with fork tines. When cool, lift each triangle carefully from pan. Makes 16 cookies.

Cinnamon Peach Cream Puffs with Melba Sauce

For a lighter dessert, you can omit the cream puff. Simply toss peach slices with a little sugar and lemon juice, add a scoop of ice cream, and drizzle with Melba Sauce. Or cut fresh peaches in half, brush with oil, and grill cut-side-down until golden brown, about 2 minutes. Then turn peaches over and grill another minute. Serve on plate topped with ice cream and Melba Sauce.

    1 cup water
    1/2 cup (1 stick) cold unsalted butter, diced
    1/2 teaspoon salt
    1 cup flour
    1/2 teaspoon cinnamon
    5 eggs
    5 fresh peaches, peeled, pitted, and sliced
    vanilla ice cream
    Melba Sauce (recipe on opposite page)

Preheat oven to 425 degrees. In medium saucepan, bring water, butter, and salt to a full boil over moderately high heat. Remove from heat and quickly stir in flour and cinnamon all at once. Place saucepan back over heat and cook about 1 minute longer, until mixture pulls away from side of pan. Remove from heat and let cool slightly. Stir in eggs one at a time, until well incorporated. Dollop or pipe dough into ten 2-inch circles on 2 lightly greased cookie sheets, leaving about 2 inches between puffs. (If you prefer smaller puffs, place dough by the tablespoonful.) Bake for 10 minutes, then reduce heat to 400 degrees. Continue to bake puffs until cracks are lightly browned, 15 to 20 minutes. Remove from oven and slice each puff in half with serrated knife. Let cool. To serve, place puffs on individual dessert plates. Arrange peach slices in a concentric circle on the bottom half of each puff, and top with a scoop of vanilla ice cream. Add the cream puff lid and drizzle with Melba Sauce. Makes 10 oversize cream puffs.

Melba Sauce

1 pint fresh or 2 cups frozen raspberries, thawed
3 to 4 tablespoons sugar, to taste
2 teaspoons fresh lemon juice

In food processor, pulse together raspberries, sugar, and lemon juice.
Press sauce through strainer to remove seeds.

Meringue Shells with Zesty Lemon Curd and Peach Strawberry Topping

This dessert is a feast for the eyes as well as your tastebuds. By using egg whites at room temperature to make the meringues, more air will be incorporated during beating, and the meringues will turn out fluffier. This recipe is also very good with raspberries or blueberries instead of the strawberries.

3 egg whites, room temperature	1 teaspoon vanilla
1/2 teaspoon cream of tartar	Zesty Lemon Curd (recipe below)
pinch of salt	Peach Strawberry Topping
1 cup sugar	(recipe on opposite page)

Preheat oven to 275 degrees. Cover baking sheet with parchment paper or grease and lightly flour. Draw 8 circles about 3 inches in diameter and 2 inches apart. Put egg whites in large mixing bowl, sprinkle cream of tartar and salt over them, and beat until soft peaks form. On high speed, gradually beat in sugar, 1 tablespoon at a time, followed by vanilla. Beat until very stiff peaks form, about 6 minutes. Spoon onto middle of circles on baking sheet, then smooth into little nest shapes. Bake in middle of oven for 1 hour. Turn off oven and let dry for 1 hour with oven door propped slightly open. To serve, place meringues on individual dessert plates. Spread each with a dollop of Zesty Lemon Curd, and top with a generous portion of Peach Strawberry Topping. Makes 8 servings.

Zesty Lemon Curd

1/2 cup lemon juice	1 egg
1 teaspoon lemon zest	pinch of salt
1/2 cup sugar	4 tablespoons (1/2 stick) unsalted
3 large egg yolks	butter, cut into small dice

In small saucepan, whisk together lemon juice, zest, sugar, yolks, egg, and pinch of salt. Stir in butter and cook over moderately low heat until curd thickens, watching carefully for the first bubble to appear on the surface, about 8 to 10 minutes. Strain into a bowl, cover with plastic wrap, and chill.

Peach Strawberry Topping

2 peaches, peeled, pitted, and diced
$^1/_2$ cup fresh sliced strawberries
2 tablespoons sugar
2 teaspoons lemon juice

In medium bowl, carefully toss together peaches, strawberries, sugar, and lemon juice.

Peach Raspberry Shortcake

These shortcakes are light and delicate. Topped with fruit filling and whipped cream, these individual portions make an elegant dessert or a scrumptious breakfast or brunch.

> 1 cup flour
> 2 tablespoons sugar
> 1 teaspoon baking powder
> $1/4$ teaspoon salt
> 2 tablespoons unsalted butter, cut into small dice
> $1/2$ cup plus 2 tablespoons heavy cream
> 1 teaspoon sugar for sprinkling
> whipped cream
> Peach Raspberry Topping (recipe on opposite page)

Preheat oven to 400 degrees. In a food processor, pulsing off and on, combine flour, 2 tablespoons sugar, baking powder, and salt. Add butter and pulse until well blended. Pour in heavy cream and pulse, on and off, until the mixture forms little peas. Alternatively, add dry ingredients to a medium bowl and cut in butter with a pastry cutter. Toss in cream using a fork. Pat mixture into a ball and press into a disk about 1 inch thick. Cut disk into 4 equal pieces, and pat sides of each piece to make a circle. Brush the tops of each circle with a little more cream and sprinkle lightly with sugar. Place on a lightly greased cookie sheet and bake 10 to 12 minutes, until golden. When cool, cut in half crosswise. Place bottoms on individual dessert plates. Divide Peach Raspberry Topping over each shortcake bottom. Dollop topping with whipped cream, and replace shortcake tops.

Peach Raspberry Topping

2 fresh peaches, pitted and cut into $^1/_2$-inch dice
$^1/_2$ cup fresh raspberries or sliced strawberries
1 teaspoon sugar
1 teaspoon lemon juice
1 cup heavy cream
$^1/_3$ cup confectioner's sugar
$^1/_2$ teaspoon vanilla

In small bowl, combine peaches, raspberries, sugar, and lemon juice. In medium bowl, whip together heavy cream, confectioner's sugar, and vanilla, until soft peaks form.

Almond Sugar Cookie Cups
with Creamy Peach Mousse

These cookie cups make great containers for Creamy Peach Mousse. You may also fill them with ice cream and chocolate sauce.

1/4 cup flour
1/4 cup slivered or sliced almonds
1/4 cup sugar
pinch of salt
1 egg white
3 tablespoons melted unsalted butter, cooled slightly
1/4 teaspoon vanilla
Creamy Peach Mousse (recipe on opposite page)
toasted almonds for garnish

Preheat oven to 400 degrees. Butter and flour two cookie sheets. Trace three 5-inch circles on one pan and three circles on the other. Set aside.

In a food processor or blender, add flour, almonds, sugar and salt. Pulse on and off until almonds are finely chopped. Transfer to a small bowl and stir in egg white, butter and vanilla until blended. Drop mixture by rounded tablespoonfuls in the center of each traced circle. Carefully spread batter to edges of circle. Bake just until the edges turn golden brown, 5 to 6 minutes. Remove pans from the oven. Then, working quickly, flip cookies evenly over inverted glasses, pressing lightly to make a fluted edge.

Let cups cool completely on wire racks. To serve, place cups on individual dessert plates. Scoop some of the Creamy Peach Mousse into each cookie cup and sprinkle with toasted almonds. Makes 6 servings.

Creamy Peach Mousse

1 tablespoon cold water
1 scant tablespoon (1 envelope) unflavored gelatin
6 egg yolks
1 cup sugar
1 cup hot milk
1 1/2 cups finely chopped peaches
2 teaspoons lemon juice
1 cup heavy cream

In small bowl, sprinkle water over gelatin and let soften. In medium saucepan, whisk together egg yolks and sugar. Stir in hot milk and cook over moderate heat, stirring constantly until slightly thickened and custard consistency, about 6 to 8 minutes. (Mixture should coat the back of a spoon.) Remove from heat and stir in gelatin until dissolved. Strain custard into medium bowl and set over a bowl of ice. Let cool completely until mixture begins to set. Then fold in peaches and lemon juice. In medium bowl, beat cream until stiff peaks form. Fold cream into custard mixture. Cover bowl with plastic wrap and chill thoroughly until set, about 3 hours.

Lemon Peach Meringue Pie

The extra couple inches of meringue give an ethereal quality to the pie. The meringue will recede from the filling when refrigerated, so it's best to serve the pie right away.

3/4 cup sugar	11/2 cups finely chopped peaches
1/4 cup cornstarch	1 tablespoon butter
11/4 cups water	9-inch Cream Cheese Pie Crust
1/4 cup lemon juice	(recipe below)
1/4 teaspoon salt	Meringue (recipe on opposite page)

In medium saucepan, whisk together sugar, cornstarch, water, lemon juice, and salt. Stir in peaches. Bring mixture to a full boil and cook until thickened and translucent. Stir in butter, remove from heat, and smooth into prebaked pie crust. Chill. Smooth meringue over chilled peach filling. Preheat broiler. Place pie in upper third of oven and, watching closely, broil meringue until golden brown, about 1 minute. Serve.

Cream Cheese Pie Crust

1 cup flour
1 tablespoon sugar
1/4 teaspoon salt
1/2 cup (1 stick) unsalted butter, cut into small pieces
2 ounces cream cheese, cut into small pieces
2 to 3 tablespoons ice-cold water

Preheat oven to 400 degrees. In a food processor, combine flour, sugar, and salt. Add butter and cream cheese, and pulse, on and off, until mixture becomes crumbly. Add water and pulse again until mixture just forms a ball. Pat into a disk, wrap in plastic, and chill for half an hour. Roll dough out to an 11-inch circle about 1/8-inch thick and press into a 9-inch pie pan. Fold over and crimp edges. Prick all over with a fork and freeze for about 10 minutes. To prebake, cover bottom and sides with a piece of foil and fill with either pie weights or beans. Bake in the oven for 20 minutes. Remove foil and weights, and continue to bake at 375 degrees for 5 minutes or until crust is cooked through. Set on a wire rack and let cool.

Meringue

4 egg whites, room temperature
$^1/_2$ cup sugar
pinch of salt

In large mixer, beat egg whites and salt until soft peaks form. Gradually add sugar, 1 tablespoon at a time, until stiff but not dry peaks form.

Peach Upside-Down Cake with Rum Cream

Serve this cake as a showcase dessert or as a breakfast or brunch coffee cake. You can top with vanilla ice cream if you prefer.

> 3 tablespoons unsalted butter
> 1/4 cup light brown sugar
> 3 ripe fresh peaches, peeled and cut into 1/4-inch wedges
> 1 2/3 cups flour
> 2 1/2 teaspoons baking powder
> 1/2 teaspoon salt
> 1/2 cup (1 stick) softened unsalted butter
> 3/4 cup granulated sugar
> 2 large eggs
> 1 1/2 teaspoons vanilla
> 2/3 cup milk
> Run Cream (recipe below)

Preheat oven to 350 degrees. In a 10 1/2-inch cast-iron skillet, melt 3 tablespoons butter. Stir in brown sugar until dissolved. Swirl skillet to coat sugar evenly across the bottom, then remove from heat. Place peach slices in 2 concentric circles on bottom of skillet. In small bowl, combine flour, baking powder, and salt. In medium bowl, beat together 1/2 cup butter and sugar until creamy. Stir in eggs one at a time. Stir in vanilla. Slowly add flour mixture, alternating with milk, just until combined. Dollop and smooth cake batter carefully and completely over peach slices. Bake for 40 to 45 minutes, until toothpick comes out clean when poked in center. Let rest on wire rack for 5 minutes. Flip upside down on serving platter. Serve slices warm or room temperature topped with Rum Cream.

Rum Cream

> 1 cup heavy cream
> 3 tablespoons confectioner's sugar
> 2 tablespoons dark rum

In medium bowl, beat cream, sugar, and rum until stiff peaks form.

Peaches and Cream Cheese Crusted Pie

The cheese-laced crust is a natural accompaniment to the sweet-tangy peach filling.

    8 cups peeled and sliced fresh peaches
    2 teaspoons lemon juice
    1/2 teaspoon cinnamon
    1/2 teaspoon vanilla
    1/4 cup sugar
    1/4 cup all-purpose flour
    1 tablespoon butter, diced
    1 tablespoon sugar
    Cream Cheese Crust (recipe below)

Preheat oven to 400 degrees. In large bowl, toss together peach slices, lemon juice, cinnamon, vanilla, 1/4 cup sugar, and flour. Let this mixture sit while you roll out one of the disks of pastry and line a 10-inch pie pan with 1/8-inch thickness dough. Pour filling into the prepared pie pan, and dot the peaches with butter. Roll out the other pastry disk to a 12-inch circle about 1/8-inch thick, and carefully place over filling. Crimp edges together and prick center of crust with a fork a few times. Sprinkle 1 tablespoon sugar over top of pie. Place on baking sheet in center of oven. Bake 40 to 50 minutes, until golden and filling is bubbling. Serve slices warm or room temperature, topped with ice cream or whipped cream.

Cream Cheese Crust

    2 cups all-purpose flour
    2 tablespoons sugar
    1/2 teaspoon salt
    1 cup (2 sticks) unsalted butter, cut into small dice
    4 ounces cream cheese, cut into small dice
    1/3 cup ice-cold water

In a food processor, pulse together flour, sugar, and salt. Add butter and cream cheese, and pulse until mixture is the texture of cornmeal. Add the water and pulse, on and off, until mixture just begins to form a ball. Pat into two disks and chill for half an hour.

Peaches Foster

Depending on your guests' appetites, you can serve either a half or a whole peach per person. This dessert is a takeoff on the classic Bananas Foster.

> 3 tablespoons butter
> 2/3 cup dark brown sugar
> 1/2 cup dark rum
> 2 tablespoons heavy cream
> 1 teaspoon vanilla
> pinch of salt
> 3 peaches, peeled, pitted, and halved
> vanilla ice cream

In a 10-inch cast-iron skillet, melt butter over moderately high heat. Stir in brown sugar and cook until sugar dissolves, about 8 minutes. Stir in rum and bring to a boil. Ignite the liquid and continue to cook until the flames are extinguished. Stir in cream, vanilla, and salt. Add peaches and spoon sauce over each half. Place one or two peach halves in each bowl, top with a scoop of ice cream, and spoon additional sauce over the top. Serves 3 to 6.

Mixed-Fruit Crisp

Everyone in my family loves to pick off the crumbly, oatmeal cookie-like topping, including my chocolate Lab, Gordy. He jumped up on the counter and slurped off half the topping, then ran back to his place on the carpet as though nothing had happened. But his face told a different story. You can substitute plum slices or raspberries for the blueberries.

1 cup packed light brown sugar
1 cup old-fashioned oats
$3/4$ cup flour
$1/4$ teaspoon salt
$1/2$ cup (1 stick) cold unsalted butter, cut into small dice
6 cups sliced peaches
2 cups blueberries
$1/2$ cup white granulated sugar
3 tablespoons flour
2 teaspoons lemon juice

Preheat oven to 375 degrees. Spray a 12 x 9 x 2$1/2$-inch baking dish with vegetable oil. (Spraying the dish makes it easier to wash.) You can also use a 13 x 9 x 2-inch baking dish, but the crisp topping and fruit layers will be thinner. In food processor (or in a bowl using a pastry cutter or fingertips), pulse together, on and off, brown sugar, oats, $3/4$ cup flour, and salt just until combined. Sprinkle on diced butter, and pulse on and off until mixture begins to pack together and you can form small clumps with your fingertips. Transfer to a small bowl, cover, and chill until ready to use. You can make the topping 2 days in advance. Then, in large bowl, toss together peaches, blueberries, white sugar, 3 tablespoons flour, and lemon juice until combined. Scrape mixture into prepared pan. Sprinkle reserved oat topping evenly over the fruit, clumping topping with fingertips. Bake in center of oven, for 45 to 55 minutes, until fruit bubbles and topping is golden brown. Serve warm with vanilla ice cream or at room temperature.

Grilled Peaches with Amaretto Sauce

This scrumptious dessert is quick and easy to make.

> 3 fresh peaches, halved and pitted
> melted butter or vegetable oil
> vanilla ice cream
> Amaretto Sauce (recipe below)

Brush peach halves lightly with butter or oil. Grill until golden and soft, about 2 minutes per side. Place peach halves on individual dessert plates, top with vanilla ice cream, and spoon warm Amaretto Sauce over top. Makes 6 servings.

Amaretto Sauce

> 4 tablespoons butter ($1/2$ stick)
> 6 tablespoons brown sugar
> $1/2$ cup Amaretto
> 1 teaspoon vanilla

In small saucepan, melt butter over low heat. Whisk in brown sugar until combined. Stir in Amaretto and simmer over moderate heat until reduced by half and slightly thickened, about 5 minutes. Remove from heat and stir in vanilla.

Index

Almond Sugar Cookie Cups with
    Creamy Peach Mousse, 92–93
Amaretto Sauce, 104

Baked Oatmeal with Peaches and
    Whipped Cream, 16
Barbecue Sauce, Tangy Peach, 74
Barley Salad with Peaches, Lemon, 46
Black Bean Fruit Salsa, 55
Blackberry Peach French Toast, 19
Blackened Scallops with Fresh Peach
    Sauce and Balsamic Reduction,
    34–35
Blueberry Peach Frozen Smoothie
    Pops, 81
Brandy Peach Cake, 80
Bruschetta, Salmon Peach, 66
Butter, Peach Chive, 58
Buttermilk Peach Cobbler, 82

Cakes
    Brandy Peach, 80
    Lemon Peach Crumb, 14–15
    Lemon Pound, with Fresh Fruit
        Salad, 20–21
    Peach Raspberry Shortcake, 90–91
    Peach Upside-Down, with Rum
        Cream, 96
Chicken
    Mustard-Thyme, 56
    Peach Stir-Fry, 70

Salad, Curried Peach, 42
Skewers with Spicy Peach Chipotle
    Sauce, Sesame Ginger, 28
Chilled Peach Soup, 38
Chutney, Peach Tomato, 72
Cilantro Cream, Peach-Kissed Summer
    Squash Soup with, 40
Cinnamon Peach Cream Puffs with
    Melba Sauce, 86–87
Cinnamon Peach Muffins, 10
Cobbler, Buttermilk Peach, 82
Cookies
    Almond Sugar Cookie Cups, 92
    Nana's Shortbread, 84
Couscous, Pine Nut Peach, 50
Crab Peach Salad, Luscious, 39
Cranberry Orange Scones with
    Orchard Peach Jam, 22–23
Cream Cheese Crust, 98
Cream Puffs, Cinnamon Peach, with
    Melba Sauce, 86–87
Creamy Leeks and Peaches, 48
Creamy Peach Rice Pudding, 78
Crème Brûlée, Peach Schnappy, 76
Crisp, Mixed-Fruit, 102
Curried Peach Chicken Salad, 42

Del Monte fruit cannery, xv

French Toast, Blackberry Peach, 19
Fresh Fruit Kabobs, 18

Fresh Fruit Salad, Lemon Pound Cake
    with, 20–21
Fruit Crisp, Mixed, 102
Fruit Kabobs, Fresh, 18
Fruit Salad, Lemon Pound Cake with
    Fresh, 20–21

Granola, Yogurt with Fresh Peaches
    and Nutty, 12
Grilled Peaches with Amaretto
    Sauce, 104
Guacamole, Peach, 33

Ice Cream, Sumptuous Peach, 77
Indian Spiced Lentils with
    Peaches, 43

Jams
    Lemon Ginger Peach Marmalade, 24
    Orchard Peach, 23
Jefferson, Thomas, xiii

Lamb Tagine, Moroccan Peach, 52
Leeks and Peaches, Creamy, 48
Lemon Barley Salad with Peaches, 46
Lemon Curd, Zesty, 88
Lemon Dill Salmon Patties with Pickly
    Peach Relish, 64
Lemon Ginger Peach Marmalade for
    Croissants or Biscuits, 24
Lemon Peach Crumb Cake, 14–15
Lemon Peach Meringue Pie, 94–95
Lemon Pound Cake with Fresh Fruit
    Salad, 20–21
Lemonade, Sparkling Peach, 5
Lentils with Peaches, Indian Spiced, 43
Luscious Crab Peach Salad, 39

Mahimahi, Nut-Crusted, with Black
    Bean Fruit Salsa, 54–55
Melba Sauce, 87
Meringue Shells with Zesty Lemon
    Curd and Peach Strawberry
    Topping, 88–89
Mixed Fruit Crisp, 102
Moroccan Peach Lamb Tagine, 52
Mousse, Creamy Peach, 93
Muffins, Cinnamon Peach, 10
Mustard-Thyme Chicken Thighs, 56

Nectarines, xv–xvii
Nut-Crusted Mahimahi with Black
    Bean Fruit Salsa, 54–55

Oatmeal with Peaches and Whipped
    Cream, Baked, 16

Peach Barbecue Sauce, Tangy, 74
Peach Bellini, 7
Peach Bruschetta Topping, 26
Peach Cake, Brandy, 80
Peach Chipotle Sauce, Spicy, 28
Peach Chive Butter, 58
Peach Cobbler, Buttermilk, 82
Peach Crantini, 4
Peach Cream Puffs with Melba Sauce,
    Cinnamon, 86–87
Peach Guacamole, 33
Peach Ice Cream, Sumptuous, 77
Peach Jam, Cranberry Orange Scones
    with, 22–23
Peach-Kissed Summer Squash Soup
    with Cilantro Cream, 40
Peach Lemonade, Sparkling, 5
Peach Mousse, Creamy, 93
Peach Muffins, Cinnamon, 10
Peach Raspberry Fool and Nana's
    Shortbread Cookies, 84
Peach Raspberry Shortcake, 90–91
Peach Raspberry Topping, 90
Peach Relish, Pickly, 64
Peach Rice Pudding, Creamy, 78
Peach Salad with Raspberry
    Vinaigrette, 44
Peach Schnappy Crème Brûlée, 76
Peach Soup, Chilled, 38
Peach Strawberry Topping, 89
Peach Sunrise, 8
Peach Tomato Chutney for Pork or
    Lamb Chops, 72
Peach Upside-Down Cake with Rum
    Cream, 96
Peaches
    choosing, xvii
    cling, xvii
    cultivation of, xiii–xv
    equivalents of, xv
    freestone, xvii
    nutritional benefits of, xvii

preventing darkening of, xviii
removing skins from, xviii
ripening, xvii
storing, xvii–xviii
varieties of, xvii
Peaches with Amaretto Sauce,
    Grilled, 104
Peaches and Cream Cheese Crusted
    Pie, 98
Peaches Foster, 100
Peaches, Prosciutto-Wrapped, 32
Peachy Tomato Risotto with
    Shrimp, 68
Peachy White Wine Sangria, 2
Pesto Penne Pasta with Peaches and
    Grilled Summer Vegetables, 60
Pie, Lemon Peach Meringue, 94–95
Pie Crusts, Cream Cheese, 94, 98
Pine Nut Peach Couscous, 50
Pork Babyback Ribs with Peach Glaze,
    Spicy, 62
Potatoes, Roasted Rosemary, 59
Prosciutto-Wrapped Peaches, 32

Raspberry Vinaigrette, Peach Salad
    with, 44
Relish, Pickly Peach, 64
Rice Pudding, Creamy Peach, 78
Risotto with Shrimp, Peachy
    Tomato, 68
Rum Cream, 96

Salmon
    Patties with Pickly Peach Relish,
        Lemon Dill, 64
    Peach Bruschetta, 66
Salsa
    Black Bean Fruit, 55
    Summer-Ripe, 36
Sangria, Peachy White Wine, 2

Sauces
    Amaretto, 104
    Fresh Peach, 34
    Melba, 87
    Spicy Peach Chipotle, 28
    Tangy Peach Barbecue, 74
Scallops, Blackened, with Fresh Peach
    Sauce and Balsamic Reduction,
    34–35
Scones, Cranberry Orange, with
    Orchard Peach Pam, 22–23
Sesame Ginger Chicken Skewers with
    Spicy Peach Chipotle Sauce, 28
Shiitake Shrimp Peach Tostadas, 30
Shrimp
    Peachy Tomato Risotto with, 68
    Shiitake Peach Tostadas, 30
Smoked-Rubbed Skirt Steak with
    Peach Chive Butter and Roasted
    Rosemary Potatoes, 58–59
Sparkling Peach Lemonade, 5
Spicy Pork Babyback Ribs with Peach
    Glaze, 62
Steak with Peach Chive Butter and
    Roasted Rosemary Potatoes,
    Smoke-Rubbed Skirt, 58–59
Strawberry Peach Smoothie, 6
Summer Squash Soup with Cilantro
    Cream, Peach-Kissed, 40
Summer-Ripe Salsa, 36
Sumptuous Peach Ice Cream, 77

Tangy Peach Barbecue Sauce, 74
Tostadas, Shiitake Shrimp Peach, 30

Vegetables, Pesto Penne Pasta with
    Peaches and Grilled Summer, 60

Yogurt with Fresh Peaches and Nutty
    Granola, 12

About the Author

Mimi Brodeur is a graduate of the prestigious Ecole de Cuisine La Varenne in France. She has worked as a caterer, consultant, instructor, food stylist, recipe editor, and contributor to *Food & Wine* magazine. She writes a weekly column for the Harrisburg *Patriot News* and lives in Hershey, Pennsylvania.

After eating peaches morning, noon, and night, Mimi and her family are currently on a peach hiatus. They will rekindle their love of peaches next season.